# On Friendship and other thoughts for Counsellors and Psychotherapists

Anthony McSherry

Published by Anthony McSherry, 2024.

# On Friendship and other thoughts for Counsellors and Psychotherapists

———

Anthony McSherry

*We have to know that to separate ourselves from the other is to set them free of ourselves.*

# On Friendship and other thoughts for counsellors and psychotherapists

**What's this?**

The aim of this small collection of thoughts is to help counsellors and psychotherapists in their work, and it may also help others. Ultimately, perhaps all of us are just saying ourselves in so many different ways and perhaps that is all this is too. But hopefully in the saying of oneself we help others say themselves or search for paths that will induce a 'living-ness' for them. There are some themes in this collection, mainly around friendship, alienation, envy, gratitude, the difficulties in thinking for oneself, and hopefulness, with one piece on the effects of suicide. This latter fragment is difficult to read because of the subject matter and I would recommend it is only read by someone who has a therapist (or equivalent) to discuss it with.

My grandfather used to have a back room in his house on the Royal Canal Bank in Dublin full of old furniture, bits of bicycles and bedsteads, things he found on his forays and bits and pieces. It was always dark in there as the window looked out northwards onto the cobbled back yard with its high dark grey limestone wall and outside toilet and sink. The yard always smelled of wet newspaper, rust, and wet stone. In a grimy chest of drawers against the window, the top drawer was full of things he had kept like rusting nuts and bolts, washers, broken torches, marbles and empty match boxes, worn out playing cards and a harmonica, torn betting slips, pencil stubs, chess pieces and draught pieces, a broken pliers, and the odd old copper coin. I would rummage through the depths looking for something colourful or shiny, my fingers ending up stained and smelling of dust and metal. I always looked through it slowly, taking my time as if there was endless time to take, not thinking of time at all. Out of some fear I would try to put things back as they were before, taking nothing. This collection is a bit like that too. Things that have shone in however dull or shining a light seem somehow to need to be kept somewhere safe. The examples and quotes are from imaginary people - but of course all imaginary people are parts of us or people we have really known - unless referring to philosophers and the like. One thing which you might find in your own life is how human beings are becoming increasingly mechanised and modularised by a society, a culture, that sees a person only of value as an 'earning machine', and also as a machine - a 'value machine'. This is something that pains me and I have not found a personal answer to it apart from a generosity of spirit that sometimes flowers between people. And the things here have often been found before by many others, but finding them for yourself - and whatever you find for yourself - is what is important. We learn properly this way.

Each thought is on a separate page, to give some space to think and maybe to scribble down your own thoughts (if you have a paper copy). A kind of space to show that these fragments are not meant to be read quickly. Although I think they are relevant for therapists especially or anyone involved in any way with the 'talking cure', it would be nice if others were to find them useful also. Just for brevity, whenever I mention psychotherapy I also intend counselling and any talking therapy. Any aspects of characters in this book are purely fictional apart from my own (which may well be also fictional).

### Acknowledgements

I would like to thank Del Loewenthal and Sally Parsloe for their generous reading and feedback on earlier drafts of these fragments.

*La Serenissima*

There is something about you that must not be known, that is to be left alone, just as it is - I'm not sure what, and it must be left that way without speculation to you. If you wish to show yourself you will. Here in the therapy room I am a passenger on a boat staring into thick fog. I once was this, on a gondola taxi in Venice one January crossing a canal into an unknown. But no tourist. Shades of people and buildings cloaked in the ancient fog the backdrop to the over-coated vigour of young-ness. *La Serenissima*. The most serene. But my anxious heart was like a stream flowing down a hillside in the clouds, too young to find its level.

But that is me. That is not you. This is where we have to know that to separate ourselves from the other is to set them free of ourselves, our own need to be known. It is part of the complexity of generosity, also in therapy.

Generosity

Acceptance is like a knife going in, not quite severing something vital but still bringing with it the knowledge that something vital is in play. It is as if knowing we are alone in the world, at best fellow strangers on a train journey. I miss the idea of presence to another, of giving so that we receive without such giving being intended as a transaction. Presence is a spiritual stance that can only be supported through some form of human spirituality since god is absent now. It was more comforting when god was not absent. There is still the comfort of writing, nature, and being with others. We have to create this stance of presence to others in the absence of god now. Our lives then must be a work of creation towards the other.

The greatest challenge to us as humans in terms of relations is perhaps how to show true generosity of presence. It is lacking almost everywhere apart from occasionally in the small relations between people.

# Do *you* think it's that simple?

# Tyrant

When a key figure dies in a family - even though they may have been much loved - it can be like the death of a tyrant. Everything goes haywire and there are bids for freedom in every direction. Some want stability and become worse than the tyrant. All manner of creatures step out of the shadows of the psyche. Watch out!

It can be like that with a 'symptom' or a problem we had when we come to understand it, or even a way of living. We miss the tyranny of its once mysterious action, the abject fascination of it. It may well have been holding a lot of things together (like a mirage or erotic love does) and now that it's gone you have to learn from its traces and the emptinesses, the harsh and the dull responsibilities and choices it leaves you to confront. But instead of learning, you could go haywire instead.

As a therapist you've got to watch out for this, including in yourself.

# Understanding the not understanding happens later – the flies get through the web

For example: Not understanding that you have not seen yourself as important (or any other aspect you have not noticed) is something that comes later, after thought, after years of thought perhaps. It comes like the rain might form a clothing on the landscape. You don't know it is there until the finest of rains shows it, as if a web has been spun so finely across paths of thinking to be invisible but then it glistens under the near imperceptible prisms, showing its fabric of intricacies and endlessly embroidered labour of concealment. The kind of thoughts that beforehand would have got you through it have been caught like small flies in the web, the big speckled-legged brown spider wrapping them into pearly parcels, sucking them dry of substance. But the fine rain of understanding has made the webs visible in the grey light and the little flies can dart through now.

The fine rain only comes through relating to others properly. No, I tell a lie, to relating to *oneself* properly and everything else follows on from there. But someone else has to show you how to do that in the first place.

**The privacy of love**

Mesmerised by the harsh light of the kitchen bulb, the quiet game of hiding things from the table covered in its check oil cloth, smiles, a triumphal shout on noticing it is the salt cellar that has disappeared, the coy showing of infant love for a parent. These are a fragment of the tacit aspects of all loving relationships that must not often be spoken of directly. If at all. And especially not in psychotherapy.

In fact, if we say to someone we love them is there not something always a bit suspect? Actions ring truer than words.

**On forgiveness**

Despite all our best intentions, a distress not peace will begin to precipitate now, accumulating like slow fine rain does in wool, until imperceptibly the spaces are soaked and the garment is heavy. That is the way it is with us humans who claim to forgive.

Yet there is still something that persists that makes us think this is not the whole picture, to live with distress, and can be seen in the astonishment that happens when we know that someone truly has forgiven us.

The lesson is that true forgiveness is miraculous. It always leans on miracles.

**Knock, knock**

"When you reach my position with respect to love you'll be happy. Because I don't miss it, and I don't resent those who have it. I'm a glossy coloured pebble in the cool stream, the water flowing around me. Although now and again I get a knock. That's what's made me smooth," he said.

"I've had a few knocks in my time, I'll tell you" chimed in the other man. "But I'm as rough as a splintered fence post, not a smooth edge on me."

Explain that, I said to someone else. And the someone else said that the first knock man was lying to himself and had just given up on love, while the second knock man wasn't bothering to mind himself and was letting love destroy him.

Well what do you think, is there another way?

# Meditation on a suicide (a note for those who have been to therapy for a long time)

*The following is a reflection based on many years of experience. It is addressed to the reader who is a therapist and intended to help them face difficulties that can be almost impossible to face. It is not intended for someone who is bereaved through the terrible event of a suicide and if you are that someone I am very sorry for that, but it would be better to see a therapist than read these words, at least at first. It is written in a stream of consciousness style.*

You didn't create the conditions of a suicide. Those were created long before you came on the scene. Something more inexorable was at work that made the efforts of others in vain. The play of words, meaning, and the stuff of language unleashed, forming, breaking and fixating the psyche is what we are up against in trying to prevent something and also understand it. This unleashing shows the others who think they are clever that they are missing something and the effect is that it makes them lacking in their knowledge, confounding their best efforts, all their efforts come to nothing. This unleashing is as violent as it wants, unheeding of the frail body, or even children, a kind of war on the living. It limits your view so much, makes you hampered by ignorance of it so much that you cannot see its action. It inflicts upon others, those who are left behind, a wound to the self, so the treasure house of knowledge and even love is ransacked, found empty. This why it is something unleashed, an impossible happened.

You could try to chain it with chemicals or a 'coping strategy' but it still breaks through and leaves all plans in disarray.

Others helps us make sense of something insensible but to no avail against a finality that is absolute. We can imagine talking about language cut loose, unchained signification streaming across the psyche like an invading army as rapacious as the worst have ever been. No assault is barred. Nothing or no strategy is off the table. Words, strings of meaning, fragments of ideas, scripts of thought, press in, removing what was thought up until then as reasonable, considered voluntary action. There is no longer free will if there ever was. It can be like an occupying army, at first seeming to be peaceful but broken into regiments and platoons with no chain of command, then just roving war bands. Just a vying war of words pressing on the psyche. It operates like a history of humankind, where the innocent can be burned at the stake for the slightest difference or misstep. That is what meaning unfettered does, cut loose of all compassion. Accepting what it has done is like a submission, a kind of giving in as you cannot see its true violence until it's too late.

Even to a stranger the effect can be more like the death of a friend. A loved one. Everyone who comes close is left marked. Scarred by the loss of a loved person who will never return. Words fail. They break off like the words of a poem nearly written, a life not lived, a shadow in the dark conveying something we cannot comprehend. It is the incomprehensible. It is like thinking you are on a woodland path one minute and then falling into an abyss the next. No wonder some turn to beliefs in religion to shore things up, to make a sense of the fall.

The wound to those left behind can be called a narcissistic one. "If onlys" occupy it, spreading like bacteria into an open cut. The infection may lead to sepsis. In high fever a person may come to covet their dead one's place. It is hard to bear a cut and would like this. We are forced to see ourselves differently, our integrity compromised, exposed in our humanity like a patient under surgery. We rebel against it as we have to.

What of it? We all die, don't we? Why such fear of death? Even for those with no faith. Perhaps the suicidal fear something else more than death? Something else is at work. The psychiatrists say 'low mood'. It's like saying clouds bring rain. We wouldn't usually kill ourselves in a high mood except by mistake. It's a tautology: they were of low mood because they were suicidal. They were suicidal because they were of low mood. The statement condemns those who make it.

Perhaps others really are to blame. The suicidal welcome death, as something has made the alternative unbearable. Rather than low mood should we say they found being in the world unbearable? What made it unbearable? Did you have a hand in making it unbearable? This last question is what harries a person. Does that mean the death would not affect a person so much if they were not potentially implicated in it as it would be just another death? Does that mean they did not mean enough to someone that it mattered and did they know that? The two questions run into one because it is hard to hold each one separately - like skipping over a hot coal that might burn too much otherwise. But we must return to it. If we had cared more and actually showed that, got our hands dirty as it were, would this suicide have been prevented, thwarted, or at least delayed? This is a question that cannot be answered. It works its way nevertheless into a conscience like a virus. It blinds clarity. Questions come up. Did they know something you didn't? Did they not know in fact that you did care profoundly? How can those questions be asked - as if referring to a reality we knew well rather than an unknown tapestry of meaning that has now been revealed? The coordinates of their world could not be - were not - known enough to try to change those. Could they ever have been known enough?

But if we go with it for a moment, in not showing enough love where does tiredness come in? What kind of attention does it take to catch the glancing word that indicates something not said, that something is awry? It is a meditative kind, surely. Does tiredness interfere with that? There are limits to how one can be meditative with another so that what comes between the lines can be caught sight of or heard. And thinking back from a distance we impress meanings retroactively as if they were always there.

What is a suicide? An irruption of the Real? A break in the Symbolic? Language allowed to run riot? The triumph of a vicious superego exacting its pound of flesh? A harsh Other who would stone their child to death for the slightest misdemeanour. Or is it the failure of an image of the self that cannot be borne? An ideal ego - an image of oneself - harmed? Questions like 'could I have helped?' will forever haunt some others now, perhaps until they wear thin with age, or with weariness like a tired smile. The injustice here is impossible to measure.

What matter? For someone it is the loss of a father, a mother, a brother, a son, a daughter, a sister, a beloved, a lover, a friend. We need to write, to speak, to talk, to weave a fabric, to stitch a wound so something may heal. Is healing possible? The wound opens up again so easily so fragile are the threads. But yes, healing is possible. It takes time. Maybe after all our efforts only time will heal it properly.

Is the insistence that life be preserved in opposition to something more profound? Is it possible to stay with the anxiety of Being being all-encompassing? The Being that makes a finch's wings whirr is surely the being that makes a suicide? The same thing. 'Indifferent Being' is not such an indifferent way to say it. The indifference of Being in death. We recoil from death but Being does not. It does not know the word recoil.

And what, *if* what if, it must be said, there is the Freudian wish that 'we wished them dead'? If it is found in the ransacked mind will it be found because reading Freud put it there? Is it that that is just a cover-up to avoid a bleaker content of some wish? These answers will never come. They stall. They were annoying at times that's for sure like everyone can be and someone may have hoped they would go away or get better soon but that doesn't mean something like that was intended. At the worst we fell into something like 'get well soon' thoughts sent even to someone beloved who has strained us beyond our limits. It's easy to swerve into 'us' and stop speaking for yourself, a much harder thing to do, to say something like 'I too am a person like anybody else, with limits'. They found my limits. But there is a simple wish too that they would have found something different, something steady to live for, some quest or other, some joy. Ah but we thought you had!

We are left helpless between these wishes. Stationary.

# Finitude and regrets

The beauty of the morning. Quiet and cool. Is there any point in regrets? Yet regrets are there. It is as if you've got to a vantage point unexpectedly near the top of a mountain by a dead end, impossible to go any further but the view below is clear. There is no going forward anymore. History plays out beneath you like an old silent film. No piano accompaniment. Is this the finitude of being, that we only understand in retrospect, that wisdom comes after the matter? Regrets are futile then, because nothing could be changed. But still regrets are there, as if magic can happen and magic them away.

If you stop and think about this very slowly though - it needs to be slowly - you'll see there is an opening here, a pathway. The luminosity of our finitude shines out in memories. Put any beloved or tragic memory in here, in this space left open by your finitude. Listen to what it says. Its truth unfolds towards you. It is a truth that could only happen in the way it happened. That is not to say that it ought to have happened, but given everything else, that was the only way it could have gone.

*For me this shows the importance of staying with the other's story as it unfolds in their speaking it. They will come to see it was the only way possible, and for the future they themselves only create what is possible.*

# Sense, sensuality, and the delta of thought.

Words and images, conveying both everyday given meanings (you could say public meanings) and sensual meanings (you could say private meanings), become diffused into a delta of associations that distributes the power of thought, deflecting the power of realness from too much insistence through any main channel. There is diffusion into a fertile delta of many channels and subsidiaries in the psyche rather than a catastrophic cut into action or the body. A delta – also with its own backwaters and swamps - rather than a cataract. This is the difference between proper thinking and the non-identical twins of compulsive thinking and somatic anxiety.

Psychotherapy encourages proper thinking, or explorations of the deltas and cataracts of thought. If someone tries to start thinking for you, then it is not therapy. But sometimes you have to think for someone else, you have to intervene to stop some cataclysm.

**Believing in someone**

Someone said, "I fell half asleep in the garden then waking up eyes closed feeling like life could simply lift away from me thinking of the transience of everything and everyone of death and dying of the fragile life of humans on the blue planet in infinite darkness lit by tiny sparks cold space on a warm summer day I whisper to no-one but myself as nobody was there as if I had discovered some profound answer to Life, "God, life is mysterious" not saying that to any god in particular but just to something far beyond me as unknown. Totally unknown. Through the beams of my eyelashes opening onto a bright blue sky, the focus fell on a small white cloud shaped like a dove hovering way up. Bright white. Small, defined, unmistakable. It was a certainty. As certain as clouds were there or breath exhaled but I couldn't stop it as it slowly dissolved into the endless blue."

Someone responded, "I believe their experience but not sure if I believe *in* their experience."

This is the case often in psychotherapy. We believe the other and their experience but not *in* their experience.

**The hermit on Mars**

"Well god you fucked this place up, didn't you? You made a right balls of it. Sure, there's the beauty of nature and all that jazz, the sunset, the sky, the rolling hills, and the craggy peaks, but it's not enough, I'd rather be a hermit on Mars," he said.

Would you agree? And if so, what are you going to do about it?

## A holy trinity

Man1: "It looks like woman offers a redemption. The possibility of an opening out into something, an opening into an acceptance, not only in her body but in her being. The angry and misled look for it in pornography, or even in the real body. Woman is an enfolding into a world of comforts, of home, of the other as nurturing presence, isn't she? Or as holder of something. What is that something? Some light or what? In the word 'something' there is a blockage of understanding that is like an emptiness and fullness at the same time, a fullness of being, of an acceptance, an emptiness of an opening into an unknown, or that which cannot be found. She is seen as wisdom, and justice, even God's mother in some places. But that is not that something. It is some-thing that is something other to what you can know. Woman seems to offer all this even as she jogs past on the promenade. But actually she is not all of this. In her there is not that redemption of acceptance, home, the opening into mystery. But not through any fatal flaw. She must not receive any blame for seeming to default on the offer she seems to make. It is more that offer that a man places in her (and she may accept). Even still, she receives blame for it, and becomes the object of anger for the violent and the ignorant. It is not her intention that in her there is some kind of mystery that is in itself a faltering because that is something the violent and the ignorant put there. Even if it were her intention, what matter? What of you, have you never faltered? Are you not a faltering being? But this does not stop us wondering what that something is, and those of us who are no longer completely lost even try to find it sometimes in a wise word, or a look."

Man 2 (who hadn't listened at all and who thought he was a real philosopher): "Could not the same be said of man, of men, of a man? Does woman believe in herself as such a faltering mystery? How can a mystery falter? Is this just man talk? How can a woman be referred to as woman? Would you not need to ask a woman?"

Man 3: "Don't ask me."

# The beauty queen

The beauty queen frightens us. Because she shows on the outside the mask that hides our own inside. A fantasy, a surface, a mirage of knowledge, of a picture, a photo, a voice, a touch, even of science. We say we don't know her, but we know what she is saying all too well. The glimmering thought, image, word, knowledge itself, we wish we were that all too well. Instead of looking in vain for depth to ourselves.

There is no depth, everything is on the surface.

**Money and psychotherapy**

Money and psychotherapy are a volatile mix. A psychotherapist friend once said to me that in all her years of practise, people avoid talking about two things - money and shit. There is the image somehow of psychotherapy being 'above money' but of course this might be more about distancing ourselves from something we don't want to think about. Psychotherapy is however a way of working through things we don't want to think about that affect us adversely, things we want to distance ourselves from. Often, psychotherapists have undergone an expensive training lasting many years - the motivation has not been to make a lot of money but to help people in a meaningful way. The motivation to go through a training has perhaps been more about finding meaning, understanding one's own strangeness or quirkiness, or the strange worlds of ourselves and others. There is the aim of resolving genuine suffering here, not just some luxurious practise. Psychotherapy is not like fixing a glitch in your software - it involves a different kind of knowledge and the outcomes may be unexpected. But because we live in a society that requires money to live and function, and to have a certain power, psychotherapists need to be paid too. How much money is enough? Some psychotherapists would say that unless the fee 'hurts' that the work won't happen properly. There is a certain grain of truth to this. You're not just paying to have a chat - this is an unusual kind of conversation that might last a few weeks or many years, or a few minutes. It is work in a setting that seems far removed from work. It can be worth asking what a person might be willing to pay for psychotherapy, and consider then what that means to them. There is the billionaire who asks for a discount, and then there is the impoverished who wants to pay too much. The answers and other questions that arise from this are one way of opening up what may be therapeutic for a person.

If we let money rule our lives it seems like something is lost, but if we step away from the importance of money that seems just as perilous in a different way.

## The therapeutic break

Seeing a client is like getting outside yourself. For a relatively small amount of money you put yourself outside of your own concerns for a while, while noticing your own concerns are often tangled up in that putting aside. There is healing in this for the therapist. Yet those concerns tell you about the client too. The work of the psychotherapist can be frightening and tiring, provoking strange anxieties and tensions. Frightening because we are faced with the unknown, and we invite the client to be curious about their unknown. We become who we are too through this work.

In attempting to 'get out of the way' of the other or giving them space, we discover how we are blocking them in some way in their understanding, and how they block us too - how we are entangled. This leads to insight, and also a whole cascade, a landscape, of sensual relations emerges for the other. It is this landscape that is important for the client. The landscape has to be discovered for oneself rather than someone handing you a map.

The activity of the psychotherapist leads to the intimacy of understandings that keep unfolding, or that sometimes repeat and stick like a warped door that won't shut. There is a loneliness about it often. It is important to stay with that loneliness.

There is no better place where we see this loneliness and different landscape than in our mistakes. It is in the 'rupture' that we see each other's geography of the psyche, the strange otherness of being emerges in the 'too much' of a clumsy remark or silence, or the ignorant remark, some viciousness, or a shown desire. The break in 'therapeutic communication' is itself the therapy; it always points towards the unknown, and not only the foreign otherness of the other.

## The fantasy field

If therapy is a space where fantasies play out tacitly, and do not become spoken about even, then we begin slowly to see something vaguely emerge into consciousness. We can see this if we try to distinguish outside the therapy room from inside it, as the distinction becomes blurred. After a while, we begin to see that the whole world is a fantasy field. Therapy is just a space where the lines of intersection of fantasy come to the fore more clearly and can come to be spoken of more freely.

Speaking of it now, it seems that fantasy is not real, but it can have effects that are real. Fantasy seems to be what crosses our mind likes clouds, storms, or rain. Or flocks of birds on their way somewhere. It could simply be seen as what comes to our minds and may or may not occupy us. These thoughts might have some meaning in relation to other thoughts, associative links like veins on a leaf, or flowing streams through a delta, or the mucilaginous chaotic links of an underground fungus. It is the significance that thoughts carry surely that is important. It is tempting to divide thoughts into real ones that we might act on, and fantasy ones that we might just let drift or be curious about, and then those ones that seem like fantasy but insist on trying to be real. The curious (and sometimes anxiety-laden) realness that insists in some fantasy thoughts has to do with memories of real events perhaps. There is always the possibility that certain thoughts (or maybe all thoughts) have a literal sense for some people, and the dance of interpretation stops, the glittering associations in the running streams coagulate instead into some clot or knot and we have to stop at the knot.

**Envy**

We are not supposed to envy our client, and I don't often. But sometimes envy surrounds me like a fog, not so often with clients but with some old friends or even new ones. There is a lot written about envy - too much to read all of it. But what is your experience of it? It can be at its worst where small differences are present. This is like sibling rivalry (close friend rivalry, rivalry in groups too) - what place have I been assigned to, where is my place, or who has taken it? A hostility emerges like a sea mist out of nowhere. What to do with it?

It seems important most of all not to act on it. It hurts to be subject to such a hostility towards a loved one, a friend, a person who is important to you. A kind of disappointment shows - disappointment that: 'I could be so childish, that I, of all people, could be subject to this'. A fragment of an image of oneself as 'above that' shows itself like a shadowy reflection.

What of this ridiculous phenomenon that would harm the other, harm oneself too? In going to a worst case scenario, that of resolution of envy through a total exclusion from the field of play - in death, for example - there is a certain relief. What of it? But it's not that simple - to hold oneself close to death all the time as a reminder that all of this means nothing seems wrong. But so does the mindless plunge into 'envy relations', the undermining and manipulation, conscious or not, that infects social relations (and even familial ones) like a disease. Envy requests the recognition of the other. Am I important too? Was I not important too? Was I not someone important to you too? How could you forget me? Questions that *punch through morality*, that seem more fundamental to it. Perhaps this is why envy does not occupy me as a psychotherapist, since I am indeed important to the other and recognised as being so. In therapy a socially sanctioned relational field is established where envy's activities are reduced by a 'law'. The social field of therapy establishes a relation that delimits the activities of a violence. Such an *internalised* social field must be a sign of great personal development then if you possess it on your own behalf through your own hard work.

**A visit to a morgue**

I once was brought close to death by my mother. She brought us - me and my little sister - into a morgue to see the body of a distant neighbour who had died suddenly. You could do that in those days. The corpse was in his pyjamas, the person of a large solid man but without life. My mother seemed to say a prayer. A strange fascination hung over the three of us beside his body. The cold seemed to emanate from his remains. I didn't know his skin would be colder to touch than the cold marble top in the ice cream parlour. Solid and cold. I pitied him, and wondered about the absence of warmth now. Walking out into the sunshine the life running through the leaves of the sycamores on Kennedy Street seemed to pour out in an endless stream into the deep blue sky. Along with it, the pity of everything, that everything would die eventually, seemed to stream out of me towards the world. I followed my mother obediently as she crossed the busy road holding my sister's hand. The heat rising from the tarmacadamed road irradiated the cold of the morgue off, but not the pity.

I put my catapult away soon after.

If you are a therapist you must put your catapult away.

## Painfulness

In the past you may have thought of wisdom as some kind of state of grace, a gift from the gods, or even wrapped like a gift into a tradition for the lazy or fearful handed down over centuries. But wisdom instead seems to be about accepting the painfulness of aloneness, the pain the psyche goes through in giving birth to itself. It comes in absolute aloneness, when we have put down the phone, closed the door, stopped writing our scribbles, put down the book. It doesn't compel others to comply, it doesn't complain, but it expresses itself in a kind of movement outwards to others. A movement that goes unnoticed most of the time. But the painfulness can stall instead, in the body, in the psyche, like a mountain cataract blocked that only a catastrophic event will move. Most of the time it seems to me the stalling is not an intentional bad faith, it may be unconsciously so, or the stalling may be built-in to a person's psyche. Wisdom is not like canniness or cunning. Or being sociable.

**Lying to yourself**

If you were to regard yourself as a lazy, simple person who accepts that the world and others will reveal itself if one waits long enough, attentively enough, there is usually something left out. There is also the experience of lying to ourselves in such statements. That is not what I am. You start to get the sense that you are always someone else, to be found elsewhere, the moment you begin to try to define anything about yourself. It is the material that perhaps defines us best. The stuff we are surrounded by in our everyday lives.

The long journeys that we make as 'ourselves' are perhaps more like a delusional trek through a world of images of ourselves that are mistaken. No doubt the psychoanalysts are correct about the ego and so on, but something is missing when we don't find some things out for ourselves - the agency of thought is lost. Even though we find ourselves back with the philosophers and the psychoanalysts on some track that anastomoses near theirs, we cannot learn from them. Learning has to occupy the mind and the body like a dream occupies sleep. It is always personal and involves unravelling our own untruths.

You could ask what image of yourself are you caught in right now. As a failure? As a success? Either one will have effects on you materially - in the psyche. You might try to counter-balance the effects of the image of a failure in some way, through another image, or an act. The image of success might send you off balance. What brings us back to something less imposing than the image is the ability to discern and think within the recognition of another. This is crucial and this is one argument for the importance of all 'talking therapies' but the proper talking therapist has to be made of a certain stuff – they have to know about the lying that happens to themselves.

### Ruins within ruins

What seems to abide in all this is the body, its alien functioning reality, the reality of the laws of property that emanate from it - the need and vulnerability emanating from an organism driven to survive. The brick walls, windows, rooves, gates, land, and gardens left behind after a death indicate this need. Abandoned as if in ruins but left for those others to come to, to take up occupation for a while in the ruins. They seem like an obscene reminder of a need we cannot quite fully condemn - to pass on something of ourselves to another who is of ourselves. Inheritance.

Of the parent, of grandparents, and the distant past of great grandparents, and unknown ancestors stretching back into a murkiness we can no longer grasp or care about. They were all in need of shelter from the bitter rain. But even worse, even all that love and fidelity fade out into the murkiness of time. Time's grim fog envelopes us all eventually.

**Depth arrogance**

The arrogant other intends to silence us. We lose our breath, words form a logjam and thinking stops. A word or a fragment of a word gets stuck in our throat like a bone.

I have heard and seen depth arrogance in others and perhaps ignored it in myself. I am being charitable. Depth arrogance claims not only the material but the spiritual.

If it is the material that defines us best it is the 'living-ness' of you which is the spiritual. Those who make a claim on the spiritual are everywhere. But some claim it with a kind of depth, as if you are known (as if you could be known even though you long to be known in your unknowability) in your 'living-ness'. Do not let that living-ness be taken from you, and especially not in the polite words of educated company.

Never surrender it, or let anyone try to tear it from you. Let the violence of others and yourself be laid bare if they try.

# The pursuit

The pursuit of property is the simplest indication of our violence. Property provides food, material goods, safety, and space to breathe. But it then extends from the material to the mind, to the world of thought, and of practising that thought and benefiting materially from it. The violence of the politest society, of the myriad of interpersonal relations, of relations within institutions, work places, extends from this original claim on property.

It sometimes looks like we cannot do without it now. But it must not be our main pursuit.

**Lights going out in science and enlightenment**

In trying to understand something about masculinity what begins to show itself in a kind of drift of interest or attention is the importance of the father as source of reason and knowledge, if not 'truth'. This is what history shows but may also be so personally. These 'public fathers' who were here before us, tracing different paths through the impossibilities of living. For example, we can think of the 'Church Fathers' ... Origen, and St Augustine of Hippo, and so on. And the women whose brilliance could not be refused despite the best efforts of many, St Theresa of Avila, and Hildegard of Bingen and many others but hwo somehow only count amongst the mystics.

I could mention not so famous other ones, beloved people, who lived the importance of being there for another person in a space that provoked confidences, and openness to the other, where we do not feel judged or condemned. *Take a few moments to reflect and put the names of those you know who have done this for you.* They are the most important. In the field of the relational, I doubt if they were scientists or if they were whether it was their sciences that helped you.

The 'father' has been what we can call the bearer of a tradition, something that speaks to us in a way that contains a 'truth' which we cannot shake off (too easily, if at all). That sense of father still persists in our tradition. It seems it is hard to bear the unyielding truth of the tradition of the Enlightenment - the reliance on reason - unless we have some kind of emotional link to those who first took on that burden, and most of them were men because women were suppressed. That emotional link has something to do with the father in our culture and persists. Women are still suppressed. It might be not so far-fetched of Freud to think of a sense of guilt and conscience emerging from some feeling towards the dead father. Examine your own experience. Perhaps it is just envy. Perhaps it is only in the death of the father that something reveals itself, like, "Ah, I envied you all along... and wanted to kill you off... and that is why I loved you so much (as I felt guilty)." Perhaps that is what a good friend might say too.

The cultural shift especially over the last century or so has been towards putting your dollar where your scientific method is, and ways of listening and being with, which include thinking, have been sidelined to a kind of mystical practise with no 'hard science' behind it. The word 'hard' itself indicates the 'masculine' nature of power and money - science programs are funded if they meet the criteria for scientific method. Reason, speaking, and listening are 'soft data'. What is forgotten is that the foundations of science in its more fundamental sense is based on the tradition of reason over mysticism, and I would say reason belongs to all of us. In the dominance of scientific method in the psychological sciences it is as if the unquantifiable, astonishing part of the body of science - reason itself - has been amputated and we are left with something damaged, as if our thoughts are no longer valid unless validated by method.

It is comforting to know that the style that some humans show - and all humans possess at least in a potentiality - of being free thinking cannot be suppressed forever. It is there in the best therapies, and of course in other kinds of work, in the power of reasoning in philosophy, in art, poetry, mathematics and creativity which we could also call kinds of free association, in the 'living-ness' of being human. The problem is it is being suppressed right now all over the world, in the psychological therapies (and in life itself) and we ought to worry how long it can take to return unless it is fostered. Sometimes centuries in cultures or a lifetime in a person. And right through this women remain suppressed and even suppress each other.

You must embrace your own 'living-ness' and take it seriously as a therapist in order not to promote something that is turning our ideas of what it is to be human into an ironic distancing from ourselves.

## 38

**But**

It's pleasurable to make sense of something. But always be prepared to drop the sense. This is especially so in human relations whether you think you have got it right or wrong.

In therapy it is the other's sense you have to give your sense to. Otherwise you make them become like you, or drive them away into something dangerous.

## Pressure

In the tracing around the emerald plastic map in school there is found the beginnings of a pressure, perhaps even like a blood flow, a push of something defining an identity flickering on the graphite of the pencil. Much if not all of what we see as identity is nothing but a poison inscribed and drawn, infused, felt, and smelt, that bonds with the flesh. For the brave, or perhaps the foolish, it is the work of a lifetime to disengage from the traps of that sadistic and sensual fabric pressure map of 'nationhood'. If we want to become citizens of the world. To draw an analogy from mineralogy, to metamorphose or replace the substance while still noticing the ghost of the form. Metamorphosis of a kind. Perhaps diagenesis is a better word. Whose time perhaps is geologic. I'm afraid it's not possible for most people - or maybe for anyone - as they are so attached to the shadow of a form, or it comes too late as we have already seeded the world with our hate and destruction. We can only step back in horror at the plague we have brought.

But to think as if when we have scooped out the poisonous substance in the form we will find an innocent creature waiting to be re-educated in some form of higher ethics is naïve. Perhaps it happens sometimes - that on some lonely precipice there is a person like that. But I would bet he or she really will have to find some lonely precipice to live on, as the fertile plains of the world would be too much to bear, too fought over. The existential push for authenticity then seems like nothing but a re-establishment of a new ideology of the self, an individualist morality that erases the individual.

If we look back instead on our lives, what do we find? Surely, it is in a stumbling from one realising to another? It must be that we only know ourselves after the fact. Or perhaps we know ourselves through the fact. And are these not the cases most of the time? We immediately switch off when we hear someone saying, "I'm the kind of person who..." - we know they're lost in some way in some trap or delusion that time hopefully will dispel. A vain hope? Perhaps many people are.

**There is no god**

The spider abseiling from the delicate leaf of the acer is no artist. She is a killer intent on her work. As far as we know she cannot articulate her own despair and is not responsible for the suffering she inflicts. That is the gift of us humans. As far as we know there is no god.

"I seem to have been in mourning now for many years. It's not melancholia. It's more of a mourning for others both living and dead who are no longer here close by me. And a mourning for a time before revelations, when living in or in denial about some facts of living, of being. But more still, in mourning for what would become and what could have become. It feels chemical but it is not, at least not in its deeper nature."

What of this mourning? What to make of it? We long for a God who is not there through which all these things can be resolved. A redemption. This is the source of the imaginary lover we may crave deep down. We instead must become that god - who else will become it? Don't wait for God to become it, and there is no eternal power in technology, in electronic circuits, in glass and pavements apart from an inertia. If we colonise Mars do you think we will be any better?

Our only hope is to claim total responsibility for ourselves. This the hope a true therapy offers.

**Wolves**

In religious belief the world of perception and meaning are different to other worlds. A statue or print of a saint is no longer just a curiosity or a thing of beauty. It is instead a portal or a key to another world that promises access to justice, freedom, and love that we cannot achieve in this world. In religious belief all things are transformed into a kind of shadow of another world that is perfect, and the beauty of this world we have at our fingertips is only like a halo or glimmer of that other world of divine love.

Religious belief then is an escape. An escape from the horror of other people and the indifference of nature. But it doesn't stop those wolves and is a wolf itself.

**Diagenesis**

Diagenesis is a better word than metamorphosis for what happens when we change. In diagenesis there is a trace, a shadow, left of what once was. In metamorphosis there may not be. In order to be empathic (and ultimately in order to love properly) we must remember the trace of where we've been, and what we've done and who we were.

This the difficulty with anyone who wants a short circuit to the peace that a proper therapy can bring. We have to take full responsibility for ourselves without any rationalisations or bad faith and that takes time.

### 'Selfless service'

We forget how much of a huge effort it is to get outside ourselves. Not to drown the other in our own meanings, activities, and needs. It seems questions arise before even they are formed in language like 'In what way am I involved in this? In what way does this concern me?' If they arise at all from a complete indifference. Some people only do it through their children. Some people can never do it.

But there is something about getting outside yourself that saves the human soul. It is not easy to know when it has happened. It is not 'selfless service'.

**Identity as an appropriation**

If we want to change who we are (what we are) or our identity in some way then the first thing we have to do is to understand the appropriation that has already taken place. And it isn't as if this kind of knowing is easy, as it is an embodied knowing that shifts and eludes us like a mirage. Then the idea we had of change changes.

Think of how you've been appropriated. It will set you free. But will cause enormous pain also. You won't be able to do it alone.

### Envy and love

Envy happens when the place of affection of some significant other promised to us is given to someone else, whether in reality or imagination. Out of envy grows hostility if it is not understood, or even sometimes if it is understood. A self-reflexive moment happens when we accept the rancour of envy, having seen its source, then altering an image of ourselves with a certain clear attention and reassuring love. What alters the image is this holding love (holding because it is only a temporary, but necessary, stopping place on a way to change) not a rancorous violence. Without that kind of holding love nothing is mediated and envy festers, its effects multiplying like a disease.

**Desire**

In the need to be desired in some fundamental way we are entirely lost. This is a fundamental chaos of the human spirit. Each person finds their own unsatisfactory answer to it, most off the peg, and some bespoke. I hope I'm wrong there.

**If only a god could save us**

We can interpret the mystical feeling of peace we feel sometimes in a religious or spiritual way. Perhaps we need to. Because left to our own devices, depending on some authority that is not above human authority leaves us too vulnerable to others. We have to believe in some divine peace, justice, and security embodied in a god. Perhaps.

It's hard to accept the horror that we have only ourselves to rely on, but for our own sakes it is more important than believing in some god (and is the fundamental message of Christ the *man* on the cross).

48

## History and science

When you walk into a new place you walk into a history. It is the same when you meet a person. The scientific mind falls more easily into the trap of thinking that history doesn't exist. A Franciscan friar - Brother Joe O'Toole - said something similar to me once; that when we meet another person remember that God has been there before us. I was mesmerised by the tenderness with which he intended this thought.

**Tar**

You'll often hear people talking about their children as being intelligent, or clever, or bright. It is as if the words are absolute markers of something desirable... as if all human beings are not intelligent. We are an intelligent species. We are all intelligent. But some must be more intelligent than others. This is the hidden message in the words of parents saying their child is intelligent... They are 'more intelligent than most other children' runs behind the words like a kind of shadow.

We have to challenge this violence. It is a violence to children. The measures of intelligence are reflected in early pieces of standard school work, then standard tests, then exams, and then grades to get into university. And so on. I would guess that many children are already self-stigmatised and stigmatised by others from the early school work, never mind the grades and exams. Some of those who have 'done well' in school etc - many of them perhaps - feel a sense of prestige that places them above others. It is a sickly kind of prestige and it isn't hard to find. It sticks to the soul like tar. The truly exceptionally intelligent people are the humblest ones.

Be careful of the tar that sticks to you as a therapist that you are unaware of.

**How must I live?**

150 years ago, a slight Danish man, the philosopher, Kierkegaard, asked this question in response to what he saw then was a crisis of meaning in the world. He saw that great ways of thought and also the religious way of seeing the world were no longer relevant enough to prevent many people from slipping into despair. 'Why am I here? What am I for? And how should I live?' became questions that he puzzled over. His answer was to become a true person of faith, an authentic person who says 'yes' to the world, someone who lives a kind of heroic life but a Christian one. I can't disagree with him wholly. And his 'yes' to life can also be found in Molly Bloom's words at the end of James Joyce's *Ulysses*. It can also be found in Nietzsche's work, who was trying to assert a new way of living for human beings. It is not easy to get to this 'yes', and it is not some rose-tinted view of life. It is much harsher than that.

I have often wondered what Kierkegaard would have done if his faith had dissolved.

**Possible**

The old guy spoke very clearly all of a sudden, and a kind of fire lit in his eyes, his voice shifting like coals settling. "Is it possible to think any more of living differently? Now, in our society. Is it even possible to live differently? I wish I had the certainty of youth and although it seems to come back to me occasionally I don't believe in it... I was going to say something that I'm sure was important but it's slipped my mind. It's impossible to think now."

Do you think it is possible to think differently to how you think?

### Lacan's signifier

"I am convinced now of the fact of the signifier, the driving force of meaning-creating signifiers in personal history. We follow their dictatorship, enchained, as if we are free. Even when we know we are subject to this movement, we are still subject to it. When we think we are free we are not at all. Our actions tell us what a signifier was after the fact. It's not predestination in that some god has decided our fate. But it's more as if some other has given us their instructions and we follow without knowledge of those. We only realise this function (truly as if it is a quasi-mathematical function used to throw objects into space) when it's already too late. We are part of the function's functioning. You've got to smile."

It feels like predestination. What to do then? Accept yourself? Do no harm? Laugh?

"A long Lacanian analysis would set you free... in theory."

Are you really convinced of that? Surely there are other paths to freedom.

**Mastery or mystery**

"I am drawn towards an escape from philosophies of technique or mastery, because they ultimately end in living out false definitions towards what is a mystery, the mystery of being here. This is a kind of spirituality. In a way it could be called a spirituality of the Real if you were a Lacanian. Or a spirituality of an infinite God if you were a Levinasian. Or a spirituality of a 'clearing' if you were a Heidegger fan".

Or just a spirituality of not interfering with others (which would have to be universal to work).

**Longhand/shorthand**

The birds move in longhand. The spider spins in shorthand.

Sometimes we don't realise we are living in history until it is too late, its grainy truth weaving us, becoming us. Try to hold it steady to catch something of it. But it is like trying to catch a dream. We can only imagine what it was meant to mean even in the very moment we are sure we know what it meant. Doubt creeps in like a chill. Meanings proliferate, form castles and collapse. Dreams become premonitions. But we keep flying and weaving.

### The sensual world

"The sensual world is not separate from sense. The functioning that allows you or I to understand anything is not separate from the sensual world of the self and the outside as it flows through us or the non-self (the other person) affecting us. But it can often be that we attempt to separate the two - sense and the sensual - for whatever reason, maybe to avoid the consequences of one or the other.

The sensual can be deeply violent, merciless. I'm not saying the sensual is nice.

When you get deeper into this, you begin to see that it only makes artificial sense to think of reason (sense) and the sensual being as separate at all. It seems like we are constantly struggling with the artificial, to the extent that we become the artificial, something removed both from reason and the sensual."

Would you agree?

"I don't fully agree. I think that sense is different to the sensual. Sense is clearer, colder, and more compassionate. It's made of different stuff altogether. But it can't be fully human without the sensual as that is what we are. We are eternally flawed by the sensual and limited by our reason."

Flawed and limited then. That will do.

### Strange creatures

We are odd, strange creatures, as a friend recently said. We were discussing how as humans our ability to symbolise through forms of language exposes us to meaning and a spin to our activities that makes us go awry. Also, this ability to think symbolically perhaps disguises the animality at the core of a lot of what we prize or admire most. The love of a parent for their child, for example, seems to go beyond love and is linked to a primeval need to protect one's offspring. We see it in the animal kingdom, and we too are animals. We hardly question and even condone or turn blind eyes to the violent lengths a parent will go to protect their child. This can happen on the smallest of scales, from subtle social exclusion of others to more violent acts. Some of course do not act like this although they could. Romantic love too, seems for some to have a primeval need to belong with or even to another, a form of possession. There is a violence about it in its core that shows some 'lack of reason'. The two perhaps come from different places, but there appears to be an animal surge to both, as there is a surge of being itself that has no reason to mind reason.

**The courage to be**

Midnight and the dawn perhaps are the most beautiful but terrifying times of day. But perhaps the worst time is the night-time midpoint between these two. Everything seems dead but also you know everything will waken, even without you. The earth at dawn is turning its face to the sun, away from what the night shows us is a vast indifferent emptiness of space. The beauty of the universe is there but an indifferent one. It is easy to place a God here, to put in place a being that reassures us of our place, that we belong, or are held in mind by some greater being. It is anxiety-provoking to stay with the indifference of the universe towards you. Many have come this way before and are now forgotten so profoundly that it is as if they never were. These things are difficult to contain, especially when the noises and everyday concerns of the world begin to flood in like radio static drowning out some other message.

It can be difficult to find the courage to be in such a world, where animality and language intersect in the humanity of being a person. I find myself saying that you must not drown in a tide of social and cultural pressures, to 'do well', losing touch with something in you that is more thoughtful. You can learn to go swimming in it and not be too afraid. Eternity awaits you.

**Against all nationhood**

My view says the whole of the Irish people have inherited a psychic trauma from the loss of Gaelic as their mother tongue; that the penal laws, and the permeation of English culture and its language, along with the loss of the core fountain of Gaelic speaking people through the famine have left a tear in the Irish culture-psyche. Something was torn irrevocably.

*Almost so.*

There is a culture-psyche loss here that is impossible to reconcile. But it is like being aware of having lost something that you never had, that was never yours in the first place. And this begins to sound like the quest in psychotherapy. Being reminded every day that still it is lost to you and trying to find it. (Trying to learn Irish in school was not the same, when after school we would return to the English speaking sensual world of ordinary living. It is *sounds* that attach us to a landscape. And most of the sounds I heard were in English but poured through the old palimpsest of Irish. It is the palimpsest that allows us to say 'almost so.')

Is this not the case with all forms of alienation and 'nationhood'? We remain attached to something that will not let us go but never truly existed.

# First question on lovers

"Now that my lover has died, who am I going to be used by now?"
What do you mean?

# Second question on lovers

"I once had a dear friend... I was in the presence of a creature I didn't quite know, like some alien species. If I told you even I wouldn't believe it. I view all people that way now, In disbelief."

**Several questions on lovers**

The experience of loss meets us with an experience of non-being that can be impossible to stay in touch with. It draws us into it like a height invites us to fall. Many people can't experience loss truly because of this. They skitter away from it into incessant talk, chatter, money, sex, drugs, making a living, alcohol or any other distraction. In some cases the non-being in loss is surrounded by a magnetic field of accusations and responsibilities, burdens taken and given, taking on responsibility for the other's life, or expressing hostile feelings towards the other. The latter in turn sometimes replaced by feelings of care and love instead to cover over the aggression like a blanket of fog.

"Did I kill them?"

"Did I ruin their life?"

Are questions people ask.

But the deeper question that is lying there on the surface is "Why have I never bothered to sort out who I am?"

# Psychotherapy as art

When being with another person there is always a strange element of intuition, or as if something just comes to mind like a picture or a feeling, or an idea in words. This is the art of it. It is not to be trusted but still to be minded.

# Psychotherapy as science

Psychotherapy as a science is about noticing things, like looking for pebbles on a beach, but not always sharing eagerly what you have found. It is also bearing in mind what others have found and what they think about such discoveries. It is not to be trusted but to be kept in mind.

# Arguments

I get tired of arguments that follow through to the bitter end, as if there are avenues that can be exhausted. It's exhausting. All conclusions are false. Including this one.

Don't get caught up in arguments. Just describe what's there.

# Safe

They have lived safe lives. Like lamplights placed in windows blinking to each other across suburban streets. Each goes out one by one. Not like the lights out at sea on small boats rising and dipping on the swell.

Which one would you be? There is no right answer.

**Stranger overheard**

"I always sometimes make the crazy mistake of thinking people are interested in me."

A cautionary note for therapists.

**To love others**

To love others is a decision we make. It doesn't come naturally. This is something so easy to forget.

Being in love is different. There's no decision at all there.

**The bird**

High up in that tree, a song thrush, his song the same. I know him there, I know the tree, where every spring he starts up again. A survivor.

Whirr, whirr, whirr the song isn't in words or sounds you could think of.

It is the eternal repeat of nature, not embarrassed or indifferent in repeating itself. Beyond embarrassment, completely outside of such discourses. In fact, completely unknowing it repeats itself with the utmost seriousness and hopefulness while outside of the realm of seriousness or such things. The indifferent purity of it was long before words and remains so. It is more ancient than any of us.

Washing across the quiet of the room now he reminds us how poor we are that we only have words.

In our lives we have to pay attention to this wealth of poverty however.

**Natural**

Trying to understand your relation to knowledge is like trying to understand your relation to a sickness you have. You are unaware of what it is doing to you or has done, and you are not sure if you are recovering or getting worse.

You find that its effects much later have formed a landscape that you once you thought was natural.

**Self**

Wondering what 'the self' is.

A 'what once was' around which things accumulate? The things themselves then becoming the centre, replacing what once was.

The unknown lies along the junctions of the accumulated things themselves.

**The hermit's house**

Nature. Does it understand anything?

No.

An endless grey cloud moves across at a minute hand's pace. A cormorant crosses high up in tense seconds hand's wingbeats. Somewhere over in the woods a wood pecker drums out a millisecond beat. Rain spots appear. Then heavier rain.

The rain beats drum on the wide brim of the umbrella. Repetition of the world. The endless optimism of it. Everything repeating itself. Marking time.

What can we do but give in to it? Find your own little rhythm and hermit house. See the ocean flow over.

This is where we can begin from.

**Knowing**

We would not say to a child, "unless you know things we will not love you." Would we?

Yet the whole vile world schooling system screams at children, 'know know know'.

As if to know is everything. As if to know is to be loved.

In therapy not knowing is always more important.

**The flood.**

Sometimes the world of us human beings is so eternally sad you have to turn your face away from it.

There is the possibility however that too much loss overwhelms our character, like a tidal wave of grief or memories of times past. Brimming over something.

You will find that time drains away its flood. And newness can begin again.

Give yourself time. And then start thinking more carefully.

**Lovers**

Two lovers completely engrossed in each other, as if they needed no other thing, no food or water or shelter. Sheltered in each other, entwined like two air plants set loose of gravity, a single cloud made of two, drifting across a benevolent sky. A dream a dream that's what it is! A dream of love as if love is sufficient, enough to make you fly. Let them fly.

All lovers begin this way hopefully.

## Crumb

In the crazy paving of the psyche we get cut off from our relation to others, and even to animals and nature. Like the broken slabs in the paving we are disconnected. A friend once told me this story which is quite upsetting.

"I remember Briciola (Bree-cho-lah) - a small white and brown terrier we owned. How sweet he was. I sometimes took him to the beach on my own. He brought me a buried tampon once as a prize. He would run amongst the nudists innocent as a lamb and naked people would be disarmed by him. For one whole summer he came everywhere with us. Yet I left him at the drop of a hat in the name of progress and furthering my career - you could say in the name of 'happiness'. He was left in the care of his grandparents not his parents. Briciola means crumb. We got news he was hit by a car a year later and died when we were living away. I felt very little until now some thirty years later. Although on and off he has come into my mind over the years trying to say something."

How is it possible to become cut from the relation with others in this way? It is as if a foreign other takes us over - some Other - and possesses our name, or the 'self'. And we follow it with all the passionate intensity of certainty. It is not bad faith. Some would say it is heartlessness.

Only emotional pain brings us back to ourselves. Heavy as lead. Cold as ice. Hot as fever. Healing as sickness. It is important to learn to bear it, in order to know what we are so that we don't repeat ourselves (on others too).

If there is a nostalgia for the past here, it is in order to rest in the place before the sorrow was sown so that it will never be sown again. So that what was will never be again. We cannot go back.

How then can there be any redemption? Is there none except in knowing what we are? Fragmented creatures. It is in this knowledge that something redemptive happens. But no reparation would ever be enough. We live with the living wounds. We are back with Christ the man.

The therapist must bear this for the other until they can bear it themselves.

**A religious question?**

Would you think that at the source of all relationships lies a self-interest?

If you do, then only some form of 'religious' belief in the inherent value of a person can change how you'll relate to others. Religious in the sense that you attribute to the other human being an inherent over-riding value - that the other, especially the stranger, has a greater value than your own being. This is a particularly religious view that not many religious follow.

What do you think?

My own experience is that we have to attend to ourselves while or before we attend to others. And at the same time it is impossible to imagine a world of no others, which shows we are fundamentally *of* others. But that is different to saying that the other comes first.

**Sadness and the father**

Sadness takes on many guises. Tears often don't make it but still have an effect, signalling that state of being that is sadness.

One source of sadness is the loss of recognition from the father, in whatever form it has taken. It can take many forms - one form is that of an unexpected loss.

The unexpected loss.

This loss is one we couldn't have predicted and usually happens in childhood. The child registers the father as always being there in a stable, thoughtful way, but then is turned upon by that same father or there is a loss of some other kind, even a death.

A client recounted his own story of this and how it played out in his life. The pattern was that he always placed high expectations on the father figure, and from his own individual situation these expectations were shot through with optimism and the expectation of love. His individual situation showed a kind of archaeology of having been loved once by the father in a formative stage of his infancy. It was this formative stage that imprinted upon him an optimism, a hopeless *expectation* of love from the stranger. The first dashing of this love - from the real father - instils an experience of loss that is foundational in itself. The cement of such a foundation is a fluid sadness that feels existential which like the toughest cement can harden even more with age so that it feels like it is of the nature of existence itself.

We think that for this to change, for this to become ameliorated, it will take the consistent, loving presence of a stand-in for the father. The therapist will have to take up this place, especially if he is a man, in order for the client to restore a faith in others and himself. Most importantly, in order for the client to be able to face the full force of the original sadness which will also be shot through with other experiences - of worthlessness, of anger, rage, love and hate directed in all directions. But the gravity of such a loss may leave a child unable to love.

**Reading St Augustine**

His concupiscence he sees as sin. His mother was influential. What would have happened if God had never been invented for him?

He'd be an influencer now, living off the internet. Or perhaps a recluse living in despair in a flat in Milan. Or even worse, a mindfulness practitioner emptying the world into a bucket.

It was better for him that he found the sublime.

**Dawn**

Light coming in with the rain and the wind.

Everything moving out there indifferent to the human.

The raindrops are ancient sounds. Don't let fear stop you hearing them.

**Live forever**

The cathedrals we build in our minds and lives. The stained glass narratives. All based on our need not to die, and to think those we love will never die.

**Friendship Vs love**

"It is curious that those people who you feel most close to, shared the most intimate aspects of your human body, the frailty of being human, along with all the passions, who you have shared your wellbeing with, who you have sacrificed most for, and relied on most for happiness, those whom you have truly loved... could not ever be listed amongst who you would call friends. This is such a curious thing."

## Transference

There are things like waves crashing into each other that never usually crash forming interference patterns.

A resonance that the transference creates - the resonance is the transferential field - has effects for the other person which draw them further into it, in which they understand themselves more, or take refuge, or change into something they need to be, or all three.

It is mysterious but not totally beyond us.

The fact it is a transferential field means the therapist is also affected. You will understand it when it happens.

This field is the event of therapy. Some are closed down to it, and rail on about science. Therapy is not a question of science but of the art of reason, that most human of all traits.

But all the same could be said for ordinary living. Apart from the exchange of money and the knowledge and attitude of the therapist.

**Aloneness**

The eery aloneness of oneself, the strange dislocated feeling of being entirely alone amongst others.

The privileged position of being with others in a certain way casts a different light on this aloneness but never takes it away. Sometimes forgetting yourself obscures it.

But what you mustn't forget is the freedom it brings to be with others properly.

## Powerlessness

Results in rage if left in the wrong hands for too long. Never leave it in the wrong hands for too long.

### An actual person

We confront ourselves or find ourselves, come to terms with our strangeness, through articulation addressed to another human being (at first maybe imaginary but always 'someone'), in writing, in music, in movement, and after Freud psychotherapy privileges speaking 'freely' to an actual person.

It is in the meeting with this other human being that we discover the co-ordinates of ourselves, the how and the what of our experience and responses. In so doing we set ourselves and our thinking free on the tortuous roads of understanding.

The activity of freeing oneself is always through a discourse with the other person. This we cannot flinch away from in whatever form it takes. I sometimes envisage it though as like two alien life forms meeting, united by a common grammar which fails them both. This is why at least to start with one side, one of the aliens, has to really listen.

**Knotweed**

We have tried to understand for years and years the wellsprings of feeling. And then just when we thought we had gained mastery over some awful experience - such as envy or worse but closely related, the feeling of rejection - it shows itself again like knotweed amongst the flowers beds. But again, knotweed has its own beautiful flower that demands understanding.

### If it matters

To accept oneself, what one has done and not done, how one has been set up, the disappointments and failings, and then accept the gift of defining one's own life, this is the long journey. The past must accompany you like an old companion as otherwise you forget its lessons.

This only matters if it matters to you how you affect other people.

### Belonging and humiliation

The need to belong, to be part of something, and not to be humiliated for it.

Children know this need even more than adults do. They use it to humiliate each other with sincere pleasure.

We carry it forward into adulthood in a myriad of disguises, including professionalism.

**Friendship**

Having lived in close community with others what has always perplexed me is the sense of my own aloneness there. I shirked my responsibility to this sense and what it means through numerous avenues, but most of these had to do with not thinking properly, which itself begins with not admitting that I am not thinking properly. Bad faith and its companions will take us a long way away from ourselves in life, even to the point that our 'self' seems to be what this bad faith is. We are left with a patchwork of rags for clothing, which announces what we are, some good fabric patched onto bad, the sowing and threads holding one to the other just strings of reasoning and memory both faulty and true. What lies beneath the clothing must be something, the mystery of a beating heart inside a human body of organic functions, mysterious in its persistence and being. It is the person however who has clothed itself in rags and done the sewing who draws me towards them and not so much the rags themselves even though they are important. It is this person who we wish to understand and ask to speak. We often need others to help us here and whoever that other is who wants to help will really have to be committed to the cause – a true friend, or also a true therapist. If we leave aside the therapist for now, without realising it at first, I am talking then about true friendship under the name of friendship here, that is my aim. For a few moments at least I will try not to shirk, even though I feel inadequate to the work of looking for clarity about friendship. But still I don't think it is easy even if I were more adequate.

Maybe it would be helpful to talk about two childhood friends. The first was a boy in school when I was 11 years old. I was a slight boy. He was the same age but taller, broader and stronger. He visited me at home sometimes and we would go on adventures by the river, finding thin branches with the right kind of fork shape to cut into catapults, paring hand grips into the soft pliant wood with penknives. Out of his pockets he produced animal feed he said was made from the leftovers of sugar beet that we could eat that he would take from his father's shed. It tasted like sweet bran and although I tried to humour him I had to spit it out. We sat by each other in school and he scorned me once for getting the maths wrong, at which the teacher piped up, "at least he's willing to get things wrong and ask for help, not like you". I felt bad for him as he hung his head in some shame but also slightly pleased. When we shared a project to create a mosaic I wanted to do an ocean wave breaking but he wanted to do a house. He followed me around a lot. In the boys' toilets he stood away from the urinal so everyone could see him peeing, but especially I thought so that I could. When I was being picked on at football by two giant farmer boys he appeared out of nowhere his fists flailing to defend me. He was fascinated that I had barely any wrinkles on my hands and I didn't tell him it was because I fell in the fire when I was three. Our friendship ended abruptly when my family moved away. I missed him without knowing it and that knowledge has slowly showed itself in the landscape over the years as it does with old friends we thought we had forgotten, like wrinkles emerging as we age that once were just traces.

It seems obvious to say then that there is a kind of love in friendship, also impinging on an erotic love or one implicating the body. But above all there is a loyalty to which I responded. Here was a *loyal* friend, who out of nowhere and for no reason but a kind of love, defended me in my hour of need. There was no hidden ironic distance or self-protective mocking that often clothes friendships between boys. What was there about me that was worth defending? There could be nothing there to him but the affection or love he felt for me. He was defending his affection or love for me, or his affection required that I be defended by him. He saw something in me, or found something in me that was of personal value to him. I wonder did he place it there, this value, and then it felt like it was my own as if it always had been there, and it is from such patches in this patchwork that we are made. I felt this at the time, and now, as strange and moving. Thinking about it more, it seems disturbing that what the person found in me had something to do with themselves that they had put there and nothing to do with me. Yet its effect was also to provoke for me the feeling that something 'good' was there in me that was *natural* to me. This must be something to do with personal love in friendship in that it comes from a different motivation to the care and attention we bestow on others who are in some way of use to us. So, true friendship is not utilitarian. True friendship is like therapy here. Like love, it can be unrequited. And the therapist's love, or offer of a certain kind of true friendship, can be unrequited.

Out of this childhood friendship comes the idea that at least the most important feature of friendship is loyalty. What does the sense of loyalty from another instil in us but the idea that I am worthy of loyalty? And every value follows on in a similar way. 'If you respect me I must be worthy of respect', and so on. And there is a link again here to the experience of therapy. Being accepted in therapy is one of the most helpful experiences. It could indicate that therapy is ultimately a practise in the old-fashioned virtues which we have to bring back to life and not be ashamed of perhaps.

But this loyalty itself appears to be formed from affectionate bonds that come towards us, the receiver of friendship, to which we may respond in kind. And this presents us with the mystery of affectionate bonds. The questions are something like "For what reason did you place your love in me in the first place? And why did I reciprocate?" Perhaps we saved each other, or one saved the other at a time of great uncertainty, but now there is no longer any need for that saving. Hopefully, bonds of affection and care remain in some way, although that is not always the case as we all know.

The other friend was from much earlier, aged about two to five years and we were neighbours. The bond seemed automatic as if it was always there but this may be because my memories are more sparse even though like small snatches of living warmth and belonging. We would have our tea at each other's homes. His mother told me that her stuffed tomatoes were my favourite and I believed her. My friend would confidently announce to my mother that Barrys' tea was better than Lyons'. We used to enjoy letting the air out of the tyres of the empty milk man's float when he parked it for the day. Not all the air, just some, to hear the loud hissing sound. When we moved away, we wrote to each other sporadically, my father delivering our childish letters to and fro when he was on his travels. In one letter, he told me how tall he was getting, and asked me how tall I was. I felt a weird feeling - which I found out much later was called envy - that made me want to stop writing as I was a small boy. But I continued to write, and then time and a change in my father's travels slowed our correspondence to a standstill. It never recovered and our friendship like many things remains trapped in time like a scratched record skipping its tracks.

What does this earlier friendship show then? The common experience that friendship blossoms spontaneously between children but may not last due to outside factors such as moving home or for so many other reasons in our uprooted society. But the most important thing perhaps is that envy can cause a kind of deadening in a friendship until it is hollowed out and too weak to survive, a lesson that I would learn properly much later in life being on its receiving end. It is such a simple thing to say then that envy then can vie with affectionate bonds in friendship, but a not so simple thing to learn. While all the while there are outside circumstances, people moving around, distances opening up, that undermine and stretch to the limits those bonds. Over time there were other friendships, some just as close and reassuring, that petered out when we would move, and slowly something began to shift in the nature of the being of friendship for me. The possibility of friendships that were grounded in a place seemed more and more remote. One begins to think one is not built for friendship and that dawning light can creep up slowly or appear suddenly as if it were always there. So that stretching and breaking caused by so many family moves gives rise imperceptibly or suddenly to the conclusion that friendships end of their own accord naturally as if that is what is meant to happen. And what at first is like something that only seems that it could be possible at some point becomes what is. Even though this does not have to be the case it becomes what is the case. And feels *natural*. It is the naturalness that we have to think about carefully and not let it take hold of us like an inevitability.

The difficulty is easier for me to understand now, the difficulty of *liking* this aloneness, that it is even maybe essential to any form of being that I would want to be, and this may be peculiar to me or 'natural' although it has clearly been formed and is not natural. Some others at least seem to function as dyads, triads, or groups in that their everyday activities are around and amongst others at least most of the time, so that there is a need to belong to another or others without which there enters into their lives an existential dread, an angst, or an anxiety of a kind that is destructive. Although I suffer from loneliness, I don't suffer from this dread of being alone, although I used to when I was younger feel that dread so I must have done something with it, to adapt, to change it, to form it into some 'good'.

But in all this there is the feeling that being alone is accompanied by wanting to be important to others in order to not always to be alone. You could just ask who are we without others and all sorts of responses will come tumbling out. So, aloneness and wanting importance are close companions at odds with each other. An unhappy couplet. And these two - wanting to be alone and to be important - comprise a push both away and towards from what can be called 'friendship'. But there is also the other factor - affection - shown in my young school friends. There seems to be an interplay then of affection (received and given), the need to be important and the need to be alone. We are starting to see a familiar picture, of the person emanating affection towards certain others, hoping it will be received and reciprocated, and along with this the need to become established as important 'amongst others', as well as the need to be alone. The need to be alone then appears as a withdrawal from others due to what others do, perhaps their means of gaining affection, or their non-response to one's own need. In aloneness there is a need for rest as well, to recover from being with others even at their best and most reciprocal (whatever that means subjectively to you). A simple side-conclusion here is that we seem to be always doing something to each other that is attritional even at its best, so human relations require constant attention and care, or consideration. In the extreme sense of attrition others can destroy you to the extent that they make demands which provoke a violence in you that you would rather avoid. Are personal violent feelings a response to others trying to destroy one's part in life - one's belonging to others, one's receiving of affection, and one's integrity of aloneness?

When other opportunities for friendship arose over the years I have often refused them or gone along for a while due to the expectation that it will end soon abruptly and subsequently been disappointed with myself for many years if not decades later. There are specific instances here but too much to write about. Some people who could have been friends have rejected me, perhaps because I was brusque at some point, or I forgot about them in the distraction of some success or disappointment that seemed important at the time. So, I have been judged harshly for my failings towards them. These are only things I can surmise, as I have never been able to really check on what happened, and even when I have there is the fact that the other never tells the full story (not that any of us can). They become polite, or silent, and the sense is that one will never see them again. What becomes clear is that they enjoy dismissing you. The problem is that I too *want* this to happen at some level, to be left alone, even though it hurts me. The further problem is that this 'wanting aloneness' is itself false if it is understood too quickly, in that it is filled with false trails as if they were true which we can latch onto or come to believe in but they mislead us. There are many false trails - we might want to be left alone sometimes by somebody we like but that does not mean we always want to be left alone by them. Or the wanting to be alone is just resentment in disguise as opposed to actually wanting that, or we just wish the other would change or we could change ourselves, and many more trails. Wanting aloneness in itself must instead have something to do with the integrity of oneself (think of the experience of being in a group and feeling one has lost oneself, that your integrity is dissolved into some 'thing' that circulates in the group like a monster).

So, setting aside the factor of affection for a moment, I *like* this aloneness and I *want* it to happen (while such wanting is a confused tangle of other things) even though I want to be important to others.

There is also the refusal or rejection of opportunities for friendship, through assumptions and through feelings about myself (and others) that I was sometimes unaware of in bad faith and unconscious ideas or motivations. A considerate soul once apologised to me for an offence he never committed, and although I told him this, I wilfully ignored the hesitation that was intended as an invite to friendship. But what was in this 'wilfulness' was not some sheer obstinacy or indifference but rather a 'self-undermining-ness' emerging from hurt which had nothing to do with the considerate soul. The hurt was from somewhere else outside of the framework of the two of us. This makes me think that when one is hurt one cannot recover properly without an *overflowing* consideration from others. Otherwise, it is like taking a course of antibiotics and stopping a fraction of the way through. The hurt - like the illness - returns better armed and more lethal than ever. Consideration is not enough on its own, unless it is an overflowing consideration that follows through on its promises. And so I would have needed an overflowing consideration from the considerate soul to help, but that is a lot to ask from someone. Some people do ask for this (relentlessly) and we get the impression then that something is 'too much' about them and we may dread meeting them.

At the time of the considerate soul I did possess an abundance of friendliness towards others but not an overflowing consideration. And this is another reason why *I* couldn't meet this person properly. It is the therapist's work to meet the person properly, and that means an overflowing consideration which must be linked to a generosity of spirit (of the psyche). In the deltas of thought there are many tributaries and anastomoses here, but one is that hurt can create a meanness of spirit, a meanness in consideration towards others. It is not the only thing that can create such meanness of course.

You could ask yourself what is friendship *not*. It seems to me that the aspect of being important to others is not enough to create friendship in itself, as the importance that seems most relevant in friendship has something to do with the person of the other, and as mentioned above not what they 'can do', or what they represent in some group, organisation, or even idea. These are just friendships of utility, although they may change into a truer friendship due to circumstances. True friendship is of the person and involves a personal fondness, care, or non-grasping love towards the other that overflows. Perhaps this is why the most common guises of friendship (for they are guises) are in the 'can do', and representative categories (I once had a minor position of authority and it was astonishing how suddenly so many friends appeared out of nowhere), as well as in the category of romantic love. It is disappointing to contemplate that all friendship is based on some need, and not such 'overflowing-ness', that there is no such thing as a 'pure' friendship and if there were it might be quite shocking to encounter, even mystical. Although we might look for such abundance in an idea of God, it becomes then a relationship of the supplicant to the divine. I have seen many religious invest their whole being in a relationship with God which seems to be based on an idea of God as 'pure' love, or loving relationship in which the religious is a supplicant. As a result, actual human relations for them are diminished into phrases like, "I will pray for you" or a kind of demeaning charity. The true mystic instead is never cut off from other humans in all their joys, failings and miseries but genuinely feels he *belongs* with them and is the *worst* of them. Indeed, God is none other than the worst of them (as we only have ourselves and what we have done to each other – if poor Christ crucified teaches us anything it is this).

It could be too that the three factors of the need for affection (both giving and receiving), the need to be important to others in the world, and the need for aloneness are the roots of a lot of the misery and struggle in the world (which the religious short circuits into their suppliance to a God in true bad faith). There is a double need here, of being important to one other, or to those who are the focus of our individual affection, and also being important to 'others in the world' (as those who are anonymous yet crucial). They can't be the only roots however, as others enjoy harming others and do not want to think about it but just enjoy it like the satisfaction of an appetite.

Can we agree then that friendship is either or both a reciprocated exchange at the level of the personal, or an overflowing attitude of consideration whether reciprocated or not?

I'm not sure if I want to agree to that wholly. Not only because sometimes we have nothing to offer the other person that they value and so there is no exchange, and in such a situation could you continue to have an overflowing consideration or would something become dried out and withdrawn and eventually dead? In friendship it must be an ideal if we need to still offer what is not wanted, albeit without harassing the person but rather in the sense that we leave the door open for them and always welcome them back. If we return to the idea of overflowing consideration, even non-reciprocal, could it be that this is what true friendship always needs to be prepared to be, and able to be? To give without receiving. We are way out on the icy fields of ideals now and I'm not sure if there is any value in being out here in the cold spaces. But it does seem important that we offer friendship to the other as an overflowing consideration even if they refuse it. It does not make us better than anyone. It just gives us hope perhaps for the future.

Where then does this leave you as a therapist? I'm not sure. Although we may pay dearly for a friendship we normally don't associate money and friendship, and so this very fact separates therapy from friendship. Money then behaves as a symbol that conveys meaning to the relationship, that places a cut between the therapist and the other that will never be sewn up. The relation still functions in some ways like a friendship however, as noted above. I have often felt that what I give is of a value that far exceeds the monetary exchange, even though the client may not register this. Some clients have. But I have often felt too that I don't give enough and ought to repay my client. We are in the field now of trying to measure values in psychotherapy, or measuring the incommensurable. What strikes me is that values are not like ornaments on a shelf which we put names on and choose or put aside (loyalty and affection are values we could say as words beyond defining). Values are instead like colours pulsing to life which change or intensify under the strain of circumstances, under the strain of what people do to each other or fail to do. So, for example, the value of my loyalty to you is coloured and strained, placed under duress, fatigued but not broken, pushed and stretched towards its limits we didn't know existed so that loyalty takes on a different form and character to what we first felt or envisaged. But this is for another day.

**Sacrilege**

It is sacrilege to criticise Kierkegaard but is he not being miserly? Or is it just prudence?

It seems to me that in weighing every option or living life through his writings, he has flinched away from taking the real risks in life itself, and the ultimate risk of committing to living with a love, a person. In the worry that he will start out on the wrong track, he has chosen no track at all but that of the ascetic. Yet it doesn't seem to be from a lack of generosity as what he has sown along the track has blossomed for everyone.

### Talking and Being

What we may not notice about writing is the sheer production of it, the volume after volume that writers produce. It begins to dawn (on me) that the main ideas are simple and could have been written in one book, or even on one page, but what the writer is doing is writing *themselves*. The same can be said for all other forms of communication and art, as well as speaking, singing, and of course thinking silently in the beehive of the mind. We are forever trying to say ourselves. Some of course are brilliant at it.

This must be why the talking cure works. A person comes to talk themselves better and talk themselves into being.

Can you imagine a helpful therapy where the client says little or has to do all the listening?

**I and Us**

I often conceive of us as in the meaning of 'I' or 'us' as a colliding of words, images, experiences or memories of those, catching in an organicity of the body, like branches caught in a curve, or a boulder in the stream, a snag that accumulates and then slips loose, then wonder what is the channel, what is the bank, the snag, the driving current if you stay with this picture. What we say, speak, write, are just the ripple marks left on the riverbed marked by the gouging and scouring of an intentionality always trying to say itself then breaking apart.

Time is the flow.

**On death**

Death used to be something that was not feared. As a child I was certain of the world of the afterlife – a Christian one – where Jesus and the saints made all things better, where some blue-clad mother Mary minded everyone, and where a father God looked after us all. Heaven would be a forever garden, where we could play water pistol fights, football, catch minnows in jars, go fishing without harming the fish, and jump in endlessly flowing clean cool river water with shining gravel beds and reedy banks full of yellow iris, and dragon flies hovering like shimmering angels in their metallic blues and reds and greens. There would be seasons changing the landscapes, and work to do, and worries, but those worries would resolve as it's not as if Heaven is boring and nothing ever happens.

And so, you realise much later that such comforts don't exist. The journey from one paragraph to another taking a lifetime of revelations and disappointments.

# About the Author

Anthony is a counsellor and psychotherapist working in private practise. He also spent some years living the life of a Franciscan friar as well as being a human being for quite a while.

Read more at www.speakingforyourself.co.uk.